500
CROSS STITCH
CHARTED DESIGNS